BOLLYWOOD

BEHIND THE SCENES, BEYOND THE STARS

BOLLYWOOD
BEHIND THE SCENES, BEYOND THE STARS

Text by Nicholas R Bradley   Photos by Robert James Elliott

Marshall Cavendish
Editions

Commuters risk life and limb as they hang off the sides of a crowded local train as it pulls into a suburban train station. The notoriously overcrowded Bombay suburban railway network ferries some 6.1 million passengers to and from the city everyday.

Published by Marshall Cavendish Editions
An imprint of Marshall Cavendish International
1 New Industrial Road, Singapore 536196

Other Marshall Cavendish Offices:
Marshall Cavendish Ltd. 119 Wardour Street, London W1F OUW, UK • Marshall Cavendish Corporation. 99 White Plains Road, Tarrytown NY 10591-9001, USA • Marshall Cavendish International (Thailand) Co Ltd. 253 Asoke, 12th Flr, Sukhumvit 21 Road, Klongtoey Nua, Wattana, Bangkok 10110, Thailand • Marshall Cavendish (Malaysia) Sdn Bhd, Times Subang, Lot 46, Subang Hi-Tech Industrial Park, Batu Tiga, 40000 Shah Alam, Selangor Darul Ehsan, Malaysia

Marshall Cavendish is a trademark of Times Publishing Limited

National Library Board Singapore Cataloguing in Publication Data

Bradley, Nicholas R., 1967-
Bollywood : behind the scenes, beyond the stars / text by Nicholas R. Bradley ; photographs by Robert James Elliott. – Singapore : Marshall Cavendish Editions, c2006.
p. cm.
ISBN-13 : 978-981-261-211-3
ISBN-10 : 981-261-211-4

1. Motion picture industry – India – Bombay. 2. Motion picture industry – India – Bombay – Pictorial works. 3. Motion pictures – Production and direction – India – Bombay.
4. Motion pictures – Production and direction – India – Bombay – Pictorial works.
I. Elliott, Robert James. II. Title.

PN1993.5.18
791.430954 -- dc22   SLS2006029474

Printed in China by Everbest Printing Co Ltd

An auto rickshaw rider steers his vehicle past the entrance to one of the shooting floors at Filmistan Studios. A striking characteristic of the Bombay film industry is that from the grime of the city, emerges the glamour of the films.

BOLLYWOODROME

Contents

Left: Tradesmen work on the construction of a set at Filmistan Studios located on the outskirts of Bombay. Lavish sets arise overnight from the dust of studio floors, as armies of tradesmen work around the clock to create the scenes for Bollywood blockbusters.

Preface

With a few appropriate exceptions, most notably in the chapter entitled *Mumbai*, the author has referred to the city by its former name, Bombay. The reason being that, since this book is a celebration of the city's film industry, the use of the former name was deemed more appropriate. Many involved in film production (and indeed many of the city's inhabitants) still use the old moniker, and as yet, the name Bollywood has not been amended to match the new name of the city which hosts it.

This book focuses on the films, characters and role in society of Hindi films in mainstream popular Indian cinema. As such, the subject of 'Art Films' from greats of world cinema such as the legendary Satyajit Ray, have been left aside, since the subject of India's parallel cinema is worthy of a book in its own right.

Lastly, this book was conceived as a celebration of the Bombay film industry, not as a definitive guide to popular Indian cinema; it aims to offer a slice of Bollywood and life in the city that hosts it.

Right: An Indian woman walks past a public toilet bearing a poster advertising a Bollywood movie. With space at a premium, promoters will utilise any available space to advertise films.

The clapper board goes down on yet another Bollywood film, an industry that creates some 150 to 200 films per year.

As India's film capital, Bombay plays host to a multitude of film-related events which dominate the social calendars of the rich and famous, and provide work for a whole spectrum of smaller industries.

A security guard stands by the entrance to the Bollywood Restaurant and Bar in the Colaba district of Bombay. The Bollywood experience is an integral part of the city. The impact of the industry and its films reach deep into every aspect of the lives of its citizens.

Introduction

For the visitor arriving in Mumbai, their first exposure to Bollywood—the name coined in the 1970's for the prolific Hindi language film industry of the city—is really just a matter of time.

There is a slim chance of leaving even the airport building without hearing the strains of the latest Bollywood hit being hummed, sung or played as the ring-tone of a mobile phone. Travelling by hotel limousine instead of local taxi may lessen the probability of the driver having a picture of an actor placed amongst the Hindu deities or Muslim prayer beads on the dashboard. The limousine driver also can opt to steer his vehicle and passenger along the picturesque route to the city centre, avoiding the notorious slum colony of Dharavi with its own collection of ramshackle cinemas, and where old movie billboards have become building materials.

If the passengers keep their eyes shut tight and all the limousine's tinted windows closed, he or she may be able to pass by unaware of the street children weaving in and out of the traffic, selling film gossip magazines and posters.

If, and this is a very big if, he or she can arrive in the internationally standardised environs of one of the city's five-star hotels without having looked up to see one of the multitude of huge hoardings featuring movie stars peering out like gods across the city which they rule, or hearing a *filmi** song somewhere en route, he or she has done very well indeed. But the moment he or she turns on the television, opens a newspaper or magazine, or goes for a walk in the city, the assault commences.

On average, 150–200 films pour out of Bombay every year, out of a total national average of around 800 films per year, making India's film industry the biggest in the world.

Casts and crews are caught up in a seemingly endless shooting schedule, with stars working on multiple projects simultaneously. Composers and music directors constantly pen songs for playback singers to record and stars to mime to. Tireless choreographers map out the subcontinent and beyond in dance steps to be performed by legions of dancers. Palatial sets are constructed then demolished by armies of ill-equipped tradesmen, and printing presses, both new and archaic, never cool between runs of film posters, which adorn most of the empty wall space in the city.

To say that the influence of Bollywood is everywhere in the city would be an understatement, as for many of its inhabitants, Bollywood is everything as well. Alongside the thousands of people officially employed in the production, distribution and marketing of films or employed as actors or by shooting facilities, a myriad of smaller industries and countless individuals earn a living clinging to the fringes of the industry. As day labourers, canteen workers, cleaners, guards or coolies, thousands work in jobs servicing the inner sanctum of Bollywood.

* The Hindi word used for all things connected with the film industry.

Right: A young Hindu girl carries a decorated water jar during a religious procession. Religious festivities are a part of daily life in Bombay, where the celebrations of all the city's religious groups spill out onto the streets.

Opposite: An Indian man nonchalantly exhales a puff of smoke as he passes movie posters pasted onto a junction box in the Mahim district of Bombay.

Away from the main frame of the industry there are those who supply the demand for Bollywood information and merchandise. Magazine stalls groan under the weight of film publications, star posters and T-shirts line the pavements and bazaars of the city, and a multitude of barbers and tailors copy the styles of the stars for the man or woman in the street.

For those whose livelihood is in no way connected with Bollywood, the movies themselves, through their trademark blend of melodrama, lavish sets and star emphasis, provide entertainment and respite from the hardships of daily life.

Mumbai, as Bombay was re-named in 1995, is a cosmopolitan, multi-religious, polyglot, melting pot of a city. A microcosm of the subcontinent, where the lives of Hindus, Muslims, Sikhs, Buddhists, Zoroastrians, Christians, Jains and Jews rub shoulders on a daily basis, communicating in a heady variety of languages and dialects from all over India and beyond. It is home to the richest and poorest of Indians, the country's most vibrant stock market and Asia's biggest slum. The city is as varied as the ingredients of *Bhel Puri*, its most famous snack, and as crowded as its local train system.

As the epicentre of the Hindi film industry, the diversity of the city has played a crucial role in determining the films produced there, as those behind the productions are from backgrounds as diverse as the target audience.

Right: Movies appeal to everyone. In between screenings, cinema-goers queueing for tickets jostle with others who are leaving at Bombay's Regal Cinema.

Within the Bombay film community, as in the city itself, all the major religious, linguistic and ethnic groups of the subcontinent are represented. Yet unlike the majority of Indian society, intermarriage among the film community across the divides of caste, religion and language is not uncommon.

Muslim actors play the roles of Hindu or Sikh characters and vice versa. Director's instructions are given in English during the shooting of films and written in the spoken variety of the Hindi language known as Hindustani, derived from a mixture of Hindi and Urdu and associated with the bazaars.

One crucial element of the Bombay film industry is that the vast majority of films produced override the divides of language, culture, religion and caste, divides which others—colonial powers, politicians and religious leaders among them—have sought to exploit and widen. In their very essence Bollywood movies must have a more universal appeal, firstly to be made at all, and then to attract audiences in the city of their inception, let alone in the world beyond.

The Bollywood formula, formed against the pressures of such a broad demographic, has transcended many traditional boundaries, going on to succeed not just within India and amongst the far-flung communities of the Indian diaspora, but with audiences that were previously considered off-limits. Bollywood has become a cinematic phenomenon that is wooing audiences the world over.

Left: Children dressed as Hindu gods are paraded through the streets of Bombay on a cart during a religious procession.

A destitute woman sits in front of a wall plastered with film posters outside Filmistan Studios in the Goregaon suburb. Bombay is a city of glaring contrasts, home to both the richest and poorest of Indians.

A man rests on a traffic barrier as a bus adorned with images of Bollywood stars passes by. Promoters utilise virtually every available space, both mobile and static, to advertise forthcoming films.

Commuters walk beneath images of movie stars as they make their way along a station platform on Bombay's local train network.

A cyclist rides past a wall adorned with a movie poster near Juhu Beach in Bombay. Movie hoardings, which were until quite recently handpainted, dominate the skyline of the city as the latest releases and star-studded advertisements vie for space.

Left: In India, Bollywood stars appear to attain the status of demi-gods. A street vendor wipes down a poster of actress Aishwarya Rai positioned among images of Hindu gods.

Below: People gather outside a ramshackle cinema in the slum colony of Dharavi. The cinema experience is available to everyone, with films being screened at luxury multiplexes, shanty cinemas and even travelling tent theatres.

Left: A drummer from one of Bombay's numerous marching bands carries his instrument along a city street. Marching bands are often hired to play at weddings, with the groom arriving on horseback to the sound of a re-hashed Bollywood hit.

Mumbai

There are few cities on earth where the experiences of humanity are etched in such varied and vivid hues as they are in India's commercial capital Mumbai. A city of glaring contradictions, where the towering edifices of modern India emerge from among the now crumbling facades of the city's colonial past, and images of devastating poverty fill in the gaps between the burgeoning landmarks of prosperity. A city of dreams, which to the unaccustomed eye appears to have been made from the fabric of nightmares, where the aspirations and hardships, successes and failures of India are laid bare in all their gore and glory.

Appropriated from Bahadur Shah of Gujarat by the Portuguese in 1534, the archipelago of seven Islands inhabited by Koli fishermen, which was eventually to grow into India's most populous city, was named *Bom Bahia* (Good Bay) by its new masters. It was ceded to the British in 1661 as part of the dowry of the King of Portugal's younger sister Catherine de Braganza, in her strategic marriage to King Charles II of England. Under British rule the name was anglicised to Bombay and the territory leased to the East India Company for an annual fee of just £10. The port of Bombay was developed, and by 1838 the seven islands, Bombay, Colaba, Old Woman's Island, Mahim, Mazagaon, Parel and Worli, had been amalgamated into one single landmass, forming the site of the miracle and the mire that is contemporary Mumbai.

Today, groaning under the burden of over-population as it swelters on the shores of the Arabian Sea, Mumbai is the symbol of India's bright economic future, projected against the backdrop of a city brimming with impoverished rural migrants. Through these people, without whose labour the city would grind to a halt, Mumbai remains eternally and inextricably linked to rural India, while at the same time acquiring some of the sheen of slick urbanisation. Nowhere in India are the two images of the country—one progressive, increasingly affluent and cosmopolitan, the other desperate, poor and wracked

A young girl cradles a baby on her lap as she begs for alms from passers-by in the Colaba district of Bombay.

by corruption—so visibly apparent. Mumbai, as Bombay was re-named in 1995, is a city shaped not by its monuments and institutions, but by its people.

The place is constantly alive, teeming, bustling, vibrant and noisy. Be it the gnarling traffic jams, the cries of vendors, the ceaseless rhythm of worship emanating from the Mahalaxmi Hindu Temple, Muslim pilgrims arriving and departing from the nearby Haji Ali Dargah or the pulsating beats of India's most happening club scene, Mumbai remains a city that really never, ever sleeps.

Mumbaikars or Bombayites, as the inhabitants of the city are known, emerge from ethnically, linguistically and religiously diverse backgrounds, forming a microcosm of the demographic patchwork of the Indian subcontinent. The city is enriched by a myriad of languages, customs, cuisines and places of worship. Temples, mosques, *agyarys* (Zoroastrian fire temples), synagogues, *gurudwaras* (Sikh temples) and churches built in close proximity to one another. The faiths of the city are kept alive, as Parsis, Jains, Jews, Hindus, Muslims, Sikhs and Christians from all over India and beyond, live and work cheek to jowl in the teeming metropolis that Mumbai has become.

Right: *Dhaba Wallahs* push a cart laden with home cooked lunches to be delivered to office workers. Using an intricate system of collection, marking and delivery, Bombay's celebrated *Dhaba Wallahs* deliver hundreds of thousands of meals, hot and in time for lunch, throughout the city.

Opposite: A man looks out to sea after scattering seed for the birds on Bombay's Marine Drive.

This city of coexistence, however, has also been the site of some of the worst instances of communal violence India has ever witnessed. Communalist politics and gangland violence have increasingly become unfortunate aspects of life in Mumbai, as the activities of powerful underworld dons and religious extremists gnaw at the religious tolerance of the city. Even the renaming of the city as Mumbai (derived from the Hindu Goddess Mumbadevi and *aai* meaning mother in the Marathi language), although signifying a break from the city's colonial past, also represents a departure from its multi-religious nature. However, just as many of the city's inhabitants still refer to it as Bombay, proving the ways of coexistence are still largely observed.

As modern as Mumbai becomes, it remains governed by the ancient traditions of its peoples. Even in business the consultation of a priest, astrologer or mullah, is still widely valued, at least as much as that of the economic soothsayers of banks, brokerage firms and lawyers. As the city, the commercial hub of an older civilisation, carves out its position in the current arena of global commerce, unlike many others treading the same path, Mumbai has retained its own unique identity.

Right: Pigeons swoop down to feed as a film crew prepares a shot at Bombay's famed landmark the Gateway of India. It has been a backdrop for many a scene in Bollywood films.

A labourer takes a break on his handcart. Migrant workers constantly pour into Bombay hoping to escape the poverty of rural areas. Bombay is perceived as the city of dreams and possibilities portrayed in Bollywood films. While only a tiny percentage of people manage to work in any capacity within the film industry, many do find work as day labourers.

Left: A drug addict prepares his fix on a Bombay street.

Right: A labourer hauls a heavily laden handcart along a Bombay street. Life is tough for migrant workers who come to Bombay. Many of them are unable to find good jobs and support themselves in a variety of menial jobs.

Below: Folk dancers from Gujarat state perform during a Hindu religious procession. As Bombay is home to all the major religions of the subcontinent and beyond, processions and festivals of all faiths form a part of the daily life of its inhabitants.

Thousands of Hindus participate in the submersion of idols of Lord Ganesh during the festival of Ganesh Chaturthi at Chowpatty Beach. Of all the religious festivals celebrated in Bombay, none is more colourful or popular than Ganesh Chaturthi which culminates in the submersion of literally thousands of idols of all sizes in the sea along the city's coastline.

Development and Change

Bollywood is a dirty word amongst many in the Bombay film industry, since it implies that theirs is a kind of poor relation or imitation of the American Hollywood. Yet the Bombay industry has roots in the city reaching further back in time than the American film industry in its Hollywood location, and differs completely in terms of aesthetics and culture. The development of the Bombay film industry is purely a Bombay phenomenon, and despite claims to the contrary, the notion of aping Hollywood is like comparing *Bhel Puri,* the city's most famous snack, with a hamburger. In examining the history and development of the Bombay industry, from the screening of the first motion picture in the city under colonial rule, through independence and partition, right up to the emergence of cable television, it becomes obvious that Bollywood is the product of indigenous cultures, trends, hardships and aspirations. Of course foreign influence cannot be ruled out, but the Bombay way has never been to copy, but to absorb and re-interpret for an Indian audience.

Right: Billboard artist Balkrishna Laxman Vaidya (L) directs workers as they carry, out of his Bombay studio, a reproduction of a hoarding for the 1960 film *Mughal-e-Azam* (Age of the Mughals). *Mughal-e-Azam* brought to the screen all the grandeur of Mughal India and was the biggest box-office hit of its time. The film was re-released in 2004, following extensive restoration and re-mastering, and was again a huge success.

Left: Veteran Bollywood actor, Shammi Kapoor, one of the second generation of the Kapoor family to become stars of the screen, was a leading light during the 1960's. The Kapoor dynasty is now in its fourth generation as sisters Kareena and Karisma Kapoor uphold the family tradition of remaining at the top of the industry.

Bombay's connection with the movies began on 7 July 1896, at the city's Watson's Hotel with the screening of the first motion picture to be shown in the subcontinent. The audience, however, was exclusively European as the hotel did not permit Indians to enter. Just a week later, at the city's Novelty Theatre, shows began being screened for Indian audiences. These screenings were met with great enthusiasm and spawned a number of Indian amateur filmmakers.

Bombay was also the setting for the first event to be filmed in India—a wrestling match in the Hanging Gardens—as well as being the base of the Parsi Theatre, viewed as providing the cultural and aesthetic foundation for early popular Indian cinema.

The city's Parsi, or Iranian Zoroastrian, trading community had, by the mid-nineteenth century, become a leader in the city's commerce, and Parsi Theatre, centred in Bombay, was a commercial theatre movement sponsored by the Parsi business community. A variety of influences, ranging from Indian mythology and folk traditions to Iranian poetry to Shakespeare, were distilled into a definite precursor to the melodramatic values of Indian cinema. The creative framework established in the Parsi Theatre movement provided the initial pool of writers and performers for film production, while Parsi capital continued to support the film industry until the 1930's.

Around Christmas 1910, when motion pictures had gained popularity across India, Dhundiraj Govind Phalke or Dadasaheb Phalke, commonly revered as the 'Father of Indian Cinema', watched *The Life Of Christ* in a Bombay cinema, and, following what he termed as a revelation, vowed to make films himself on Indian themes. He spent the following two months watching every film he could and studying any literature available on film technique. He is said to have declared, "Like The Life of Christ, I shall make pictures on Rama and Krishna."

Using his life insurance as collateral he took out a loan and travelled to England in February 1912 to purchase equipment and to learn more about the process of filmmaking. He raised finance for his first film *Raja Harishchandra* (King Harishchandra), based on a story from the Indian epic, the *Mahabharata*, from a photographic equipment dealer by making a trick film entitled *Birth of a Pea Plant*, which he shot one frame a day to show the growth of the plant.

On 3 May 1913, at Bombay's Coronation Cinematographic Theatre, Phalke's efforts reached fruition when *Raja Harishchandra,* widely regarded as the first Indian feature film, opened for commercial screening with both Hindi and English subtitles in order to attract the widest possible audience. With the opening of *Raja Harishchandra*, Phalke had not only produced the first Indian feature film, but he had set in motion what would prove to be a long-standing popular genre in Indian cinema known as 'Mythologicals' (films based on Hindu mythology).

The initial response to the film was not overwhelming; people felt the admission charges too high for a mere 40 minutes of entertainment. So at Bombay screenings Phalke hired dancing girls, and invited the leading newspapers to free shows. The press gave *Raja Harishchandra* rave reviews, and Phalke, having saved the film from oblivion, learned the importance of effective promotion and distribution.

In 1918, Phalke established the Hindustan Cinema Films Company, which was the first studio to handle its own distribution, with offices in Madras and Bombay. While Phalke remained the studio's primary filmmaker, a further six directors made films under its patronage. In 1933, the studio which had till date produced some 44 silent features, a number of short films and one talkie, failed and closed. Dhundiraj Govind Phalke, the pioneer of Indian cinema, died a pauper in 1944, his work in the formative years of Indian cinema, forgotten. Only in 1966, with the establishment of the Dadasaheb Phalke Lifetime Achievement Awards to honour ground breaking initiatives in cinema, was his contribution to the industry recognised.

Bombay had, by the mid 1920's, become the capital of Indian film production. What Phalke had struggled to get off the ground in 1913 had grown into an industry with its own infrastructure of studios, theatres and processing labs. By the early 1930's, film production competed with textiles as the city's most significant business.

In 1931, the first Hindi film with sound, *Alam Ara* (Beauty of the World), based on a popular Parsi Theatre production, was released. With it came the first of song and dance, fundamentals of popular Indian cinema. Within a decade of the arrival of talkies, the screening of foreign films fell to a mere ten per cent of the market, while the Bombay industry thrived and developed.

Yet the arrival of sound brought with it a new set of dilemmas. Bombay itself was, and is, a polyglot city, with Marathi and Gujarati being the most dominant tongues. Across India, many languages and a multitude of dialects are spoken. Bombay film makers, therefore, faced the immediate predicament of choosing in which language films should be made to maximise the target audience.

The variety of Hindi known as Hindustani was decided upon since it was spoken in some form or at least understood by most North Indians, and thus Bombay became the only city whose film industry's productions were made in a language other than its own dominant tongue.

This page and right: The gateways of Bombay's numerous film studios are simple, without any fancy signages.

STUDIO
NO PARKING INFRONT OF THE GATE
RESTRICTED ENTRY FOR
AUTO RICKSHAWS AND TAXI
NO ENTRY WITHOUT CINE
UNIONS IDENTITY CARD.
TRESPASSER WILL BE
PROCECUTED.
— BY ORDER
TIME
8 A.M. TO 11 A.M.
1 P.M. TO 3 P.M.
6 P.M. TO 8 P.M.

While the use of Hindustani may have widened the potential audience for films, it did exclude many performers of the silent era as they didn't have sufficient command of the language. Actresses had been mainly Anglo-Indians since their mixed heritage freed them from the traditions of Indian society, where public performance by women was associated with courtesan culture and even prostitution. Many actors of the silent era had been wrestlers and circus performers, and the arrival of sound largely excluded them from the industry as performers were now required not only to act but also to dance and sing in Hindustani.

In 1935, with the advent of the lip-synch technique, another unique Bombay film industry institution came into being, that of the playback singer. This meant that songs could be recorded by professional singers and the actors were then required to simply mime to the singer's performance. The introduction of the technique also meant that songs could be used to promote new films prior to their release; another enduring practice of the Bombay industry. Playback singers became stars themselves, and in the case of male vocalists Kishore Kumar, Mukesh and Mohammad Rafi, and female singers Lata Mangeshkar and her younger sister Asha Bhosle, their fame proved more enduring than many of the actors and actresses who mimed to their songs.

Up until the outbreak of World War II in 1939, studios, who funded productions in their entirety, ran the Bombay film industry and had technicians, directors and actors as contracted employees. Of the Bombay studios established during this period, Bombay Talkies and Imperial Films Company played key roles in the development of the industry.

Imperial Films, founded in 1926 by Ardeshir Irani, was renowned for its technological innovations, producing the first talkie *Alam Ara* and the first indigenously processed colour film *Kisan Kanya* (Farmer's Daughter) in 1937. Two of the artistes employed by the studio were the two acolytes of the silent era—Sulochana (born Ruby Myers) and Zubeida who played the lead role in *Alam Ara*. Imperial Films also signed the then young actor Prithviraj Kapoor, a leading actor in post-independence Indian cinema and head of what was to become Bollywood's first and most enduring acting dynasty.

In 1934, Himanshu Rai, credited with bringing technical sophistication to Indian cinema, along with the first lady of the Indian screen, Devika Rani, founded Bombay Talkies, the first Indian movie company to be registered as a public limited company. Technical eminence aside, Bombay Talkies was the first studio to tackle social reformist themes, forging the way with *Achhut Kanya* (The Untouchable Girl) in 1937. It was directed by Franz Osten, the German director who directed all Bombay Talkies productions up until his internment by the British at the start of World War II. *Achhut Kanya*, the love story between an untouchable girl and a Brahmin (Hinduism's highest caste) boy was both a critical and commercial success. Bombay Talkies introduced some of the biggest names of post-independence Indian cinema. Dev Anand, Raj Kapoor, Ashok Kumar and Dilip Kumar all emerged from the studio's stable.

What is referred to as 'The Studio Era' in the history of Indian cinema, represents a relatively short period in the development of what would go on to be popularly known as Bollywood. Unlike their Hollywood counterparts, the Indian studios did not succeed in monopolising the industry, carving it up between a select few, nor did they control their own distribution and exhibition. Poor distribution often leads to box-office failure, a series of failures leading to the studio's closure.

With the outbreak of World War II in 1939, India, as a British colony, was drawn into the conflict. Indians were divided over support for the war, and during this period of frustration emerged two distinct movements which came at what was to be the climax of India's struggle for independence from British colonial rule: Mahatma Gandhi's non-violent 'Quit India' civil disobedience movement, and Bengali nationalist Shubas Chandra Bose's Indian National Army which supported the German, Italian and Japanese war effort against the British. Amidst these two opposing strategies with a shared agenda, a third movement with its own agenda gained momentum in the form of the All India Muslim League with Mohammad Ali Jinnah at the helm calling for an independent Pakistan for India's Muslims.

Below: Bollywood actress Kareena Kapoor (in blue) performs a song and dance routine during a film festival. She is from the fourth generation of the famous Kapoor family to have become a star of the screen in Hindi films.

In terms of the impact of the war on the film industry, it both temporarily altered the chemistry of the films produced, and permanently altered the economic structure of the industry.

The film advisory board, established by the colonial government in India, monopolised the distribution of raw film stock, and rigorously censored any films alluding to support of the Indian independence movement, while giving preference to films supporting the war effort, resulting in the production of a glut of war movies.

Wartime shortages of essential commodities led to a thriving black market, the profits of which were increasingly invested and laundered in film production. The input of black-market earnings into the film industry effectively saw the end of 'The Studio Era', since studios were unable to match salaries offered to stars by independent producers. The dominance of the independent producer has, since the years of World War II, been a prevailing characteristic of the Bombay film industry.

On 15 August 1947, India gained its independence from British rule, but along with it came the partition of the subcontinent to create an independent Pakistan for India's Muslims, whom as 25 per cent of the total population, feared, or had been taught to fear, marginalisation in a democratic system where they were the minority. During the period of British rule in India, the colonial power had operated a policy of 'Divide and Rule' which had, according to some historians, created the segregation of the two communities, while others contend that the divide between Hindus and Muslims was simply deepened as a result of colonial policy.

The creation of Pakistan had been discussed for several years, although what shape it should take had never been clearly decided. A major problem of the Pakistan question was that Muslims were in the majority on two opposite sides of the country, meaning that the country would have two territories separated by approximately 1,500 km of Indian territory. Yet the more difficult question came in areas where neither Hindus nor Muslims were in the majority, and was further complicated by the fact that any partition of Punjab province was unacceptable to the Sikh community since the province is the heartland of their faith. The partition of British India as it finally happened in 1947 was rushed through by the departing colonials, the map of the subcontinent was redrawn in one month, and neither side was truly satisfied with the result.

In the two months following independence, the biggest and quickest migration of the twentieth century took place, with 10–15 million people migrating into the two newly-formed countries. The fact that independence was granted to both India and Pakistan prior to the implementation of partition had disastrous consequences, although communal tensions had erupted and widespread rioting had ensued long before the demarcation was complete. Managing and policing such a vast population exchange was an impossible task for the governments of the two infant nations. A break-down in law and order ensued, leading to the death of at least one million people—Hindus, Muslims and Sikhs—in widespread and vicious rioting. The legacy of partition left deep scars on both nations, and territorial disputes have led the two nations into two wars and tense relations ever since.

In terms of the impact of partition upon the Bombay film industry, it did benefit from the weakening of the Calcutta-based Bengali language film industry and the Lahore-based Punjabi language industry. Both Punjab and Bengal had been divided between the two newly formed countries and had been the sites of the worst of the horrors of partition. The markets for these two industries had also been divided, and hostile relations between India and Pakistan made any form of cultural exchange difficult if not impossible. As a result, the Hindi film industry of Bombay assumed an even more 'National' position in independent India than it had done in the years leading up to the departure of the British. It also remained a truly secular industry, a fact that has endured to the present day despite the increasing marginalisation of Muslims elsewhere in Indian society.

Left: Bollywood movie mogul Yash Chopra received the 2001 Dadasaheb Phalke Award. His career in the film industry spans over 50 years, starting as an assistant in his elder brother's production company, B.R. Films. Today, he has become one of the most successful directors/producers in the Hindi film industry.

Following partition, the population of India's major cities swelled as the newly independent country struggled to accommodate refugees who had fled their homes in areas that fell in what had become East Pakistan (which became Bangladesh in 1971) and West Pakistan (Pakistan). Bombay was no exception. The influx of immigrants into Bombay from territories ceded to Pakistan, however, brought with it some of the most prominent figures of post-independence cinema, although pre-independence talents such as the eminent singer/actress Noorjahan and music director Ghulam Haider migrated to Pakistan.

In the aftermath of partition, the government of India channelled resources into the development and promotion of a Sanskrit-based variety of the Hindi language. As a result Urdu, which had become the national language of Pakistan, suffered greatly in terms of literature and scholarship throughout most of the country. The Bombay film industry, however, continued its tradition of making movies in Hindustani, the Hindi-Urdu hybrid. Urdu poets became lyricists and dialogue writers in the industry and as a result it became one area in independent India where the rich, poetic traditions of Urdu continued to blossom through the dialogues and song lyrics, infused with the metaphors and style inherited from its Arabic and Persian connections.

Independence brought with it hardships for the industry, as against a backdrop of the traumas of partition, food shortages and a refugee crisis, entertainment was not a major concern for the government or for the majority of the population. As the newly-formed government faced the phenomenal tasks of building a nation, developing the economy and infrastructure and programmes for industrialisation and food self-sufficiency, naturally the film industry was a low priority when it came to the allocation of resources. Shortages of basic building materials precipitated a ban on theatre construction in 1948, and a hike in entertainment tax along with the introduction of a whole array of new duties levied on the distribution and exhibition of films, rang in hard times for the industry. These difficulties were further compounded by the censorship and classification of films. The government of independent India headed by Jawaharlal Nehru became even more stringent than it had been under colonial rule.

In addition to this, in the decade following independence, the government, as part of measures to shake off any cultural legacy of India's colonial past and further cement a sense of nationhood, set about the promotion of Indian classical forms of music and dance. Meanwhile, the songs and routines of films became the subject of parliamentary debate and objects of criticism for what was seen as their overtly Western influences.

By the 1950's, a theatre movement formed in 1943—the Indian People's Theatre Association (IPTA) with connections to the Communist Party of India—had become more influential in the film industry. Many who had worked in the movement in the early years now worked in films, so the ITPA's social reformist agenda of promoting the rights and dignity of the working classes, and highlighting the exploitation of workers by the capitalist system, had also made inroads into films. The influence of the IPTA along with the imprint left by visiting Italian filmmakers at the first international film festival of India in 1952, saw an increase in respect for elements of social realism in films, albeit in the Bombay tradition of absorption and reinterpretation. During this period, selected Bombay filmmakers began dipping their toes for the first time into the 'Crime Thriller' genre.

As Nehru's government was cementing together a nation and a sense of national identity in the wake of independence and partition, several filmmakers responded with the production of films with a patriotic flavour.

Left: A poster shows a montage of vintage Bollywood film posters. Posters from old Hindi films have become valuable collectors items and the subject of exhibitions both locally and overseas.

The year 1955 saw the release of Raj Kapoor's *Shree 420** (Mr. 420 or The Gentleman Cheat) in which Kapoor plays the role of a Chaplinesque tramp, transformed from a simple and honest man into a fraudster after arriving in Bombay with only his aspirations, his B.A. degree and a medal for honesty, only to find that all are worthless on the harsh streets of the city. The movie's main song, steeped in patriotism, is still a much-loved and often quoted maxim to the spirit of Indian identity and its ability to absorb foreign influence yet remain in tact.

Mera joota hai Japani
Ye pataloon inglistani
Sar pe lal topi roosi
Phir bhi dil hai hindustani

My shoes are Japanese,
These trousers are English,
on my head's a red Russian hat,
but still my heart is Indian!

The theme of the film may also be seen as a metaphor for the choices facing the citizens of the newly independent India. Its representation of the city as a place of opportunity with an underbelly of burgeoning crime provides an accurate picture of Indian cities in the post-independence era. Yet for all its subtext, *Shree 420* remains an upbeat and entertaining movie, which has taken its place among the classics of Indian cinema.

*named after section 420 of the Indian penal code governing fraud and deception

The Oscar-nominated *Mother India* released in 1957, directed by Mehboob Khan, starring Nargis, her future husband Sunil Dutt, and Raj Kumar, is probably the most famous and critically acclaimed film of the era. Rich in metaphors of the partition of India and a nation struggling towards self-sufficiency, the story narrates the life of the protagonist Radha, a poor peasant, as she works to raise her two sons after her husband deserted the family following an accident in which he lost both his arms. This epic saga of the sufferings of an Indian peasant woman is regarded as one of the most important films in the history of Indian cinema, often being regarded as the Indian *Gone with the Wind* in terms of its significance in the history and development of popular Indian cinema. The film was an enormous success amongst audiences and critics alike; one such review appearing in *Filmfare* magazine in 1957 encapsulates both the power of the movie and its significance for the film industry. 'Every once in a while comes a motion picture which helps the industry to cover the mile to the milestone. Mehboob's magnum opus, *Mother India*, which was released in the fortnight is one such film.'

After over a decade in the making, a complete change of cast and a budget of US$3 million (the average cost for a film produced in India at the time being US$200,000), K. Asif's epic masterpiece *Mughal-e-Azam* (The Age of Mughals) was released in 1960. Premiering simultaneously in 150 theatres across India, the film, based on the well-known legend of the love between Prince Salim (who later

became Emperor Jahangir) and Anarkali, the court dancer, became the biggest money grosser at that time. The legend has been brought to the screen several times in various Indian languages, most notably in *Anarkali*, a 1953 Hindi version directed by Nandlal Jaswantlal. Yet Asif's *Mughal-e-Azam*, starring Prithviraj Kapoor as Emperor Akbar, Dilip Kumar as Prince Salim and Madhubala as Anarkali, is widely acknowledged as the definitive version. In his treatment of the story, Asif departed from the legend in providing Anarkali with a means of escape from her death sentence which the original did not; he gave viewers a happier ending. Furthermore, its matter of fact treatment of religion promoted religious tolerance without making it a central theme. In the retelling of an indigenous legend, *Mughal-e-Azam* presented the issues of patriotism and secularism by drawing from a segment in India's own rich history, namely the reign of Emperor Akbar, renowned as the most religiously tolerant of the Mughal emperors.

Widely accorded the status of the Golden Age of Hindi cinema, the 1950's and 1960's saw the release of films that are revered as classics, exalted as works of integrity and true creativity, and while many in the industry acknowledge the work of the early pioneers, the films of that era represent the true heritage of the current industry.

Movies from this period are also increasingly subject to remakes and re-releases. *Mughal-e-Azam* was colourised, re-mastered and re-released in 2004 to be a major box-office hit again. A remake of *Devdas*, based on the Bengali novel by Sarat

Chandra Chatterjee committed to film in 1935 and then again in 1955, wooed audiences the world over in its 2002 highest-budget-Hindi-movie incarnation starring Shah Rukh Khan, Aishwarya Rai and Madhuri Dixit. The list of remakes of earlier Hindi movies is lengthening each year, giving both an indication of the esteem in which films of this era are held, and the Bombay film industry's propensity for introspection.

A sense of hope for the future and a faith in the justice and benevolence of the state were elements in the fabric of films in the post-independence era right up until the end of the 1960's, but with the arrival of the 1970's, optimism ran dry in India, and the nature of movies and heroes was set to change.

The 1970's were turbulent times across India. The economy had been set reeling by the war with Pakistan in 1971, and the hardships were further compounded in 1972 and 1973 with widespread drought and food shortages. Disaffection with the government was widespread and demonstrations, heavily handled by police and security forces, disintegrating into riots were an almost daily occurrence.

By 1975, the whole country was in ferment, and brought to boiling point when the High Court of Allahabad, in the state of Uttar Pradesh found the then Prime Minister Indira Gandhi guilty of election fraud in her 1971 campaign. Calls for her resignation resounded from all quarters including members of her own Congress Party. Following a mass rally demonstrating against her remaining in office, she declared a State of Emergency on

Left: Visitors view movie stills and posters at an exhibition at Bombay's Jehangir Art Gallery. Memorabilia from early Hindi movies have become valuable collectors items.

Above: All tastes and pockets are catered to by Bollywood. Canteens at the film studios are where actors, crew and extras gather during breaks between shoots.

26 June 1975, invoking article 352 of the Indian Constitution, and granting herself extraordinary powers. Civil liberties were suspended and the press fettered as over 100,000 people were arrested and detained without trial. During the Emergency, Indira's son Sanjay Gandhi managed a population control programme, involving the forced sterilisation of millions of men and women, mostly from the poorer sections of society. He was also responsible for the displacement of thousands of people in slum clearance projects. The Emergency lasted until Indira Gandhi called for national elections to be held in March 1977, in which an overwhelming majority defeated her and the Congress Party.

During these years of turmoil, the subject of films changed its focus from the family and domestic issues, to the bigger picture of the problems faced by the common people in a nation where the law could not be relied upon to deliver justice, and where problems of unemployment and rising crime rates went unchecked. The movies, in reflection of the times, became more violent, and these troubled years called for a different kind of hero.

In *Mother India,* the image of an angry young man taking the law into his own hands had emerged in the form of Radha's youngest son Briju played by Sunil Dutt, but in 1973 with the release of *Zanjeer* (Chains) directed by Prakash Mehra, Amitabh Bachchan defined the role and set the course of the Hindi film industry on a different track. The movie represented a dramatic departure from the earlier romantic themes, and the new, redefined, working-man's hero found a sympathetic audience in the prevailing climate of disillusionment and discontent. *Zanjeer* catapulted Bachchan, who after a series of box office failures was preparing to pack up his bags and return to his native Allahabad if this film also failed, to a level of stardom from which he has yet to tumble.

The impact of *Zanjeer* on the industry was enormous, but the movie of the era, still playing to packed houses 30 years after its initial release in 1975 is *Sholay* (Flames). Renowned as India's best known 'curry western', the film included the rugged scenery, bandits on horseback and fierce gunfights of American spaghetti westerns but the inclusion of romance, comedy and songs added a distinctly Bombay flavour. Directed by Ramesh Sippy and starring Amitabh Bachchan, Dharmendra, Sanjeev Kumar, Hema Malini and Jaya Badhuri, *Sholay* struck a nerve with audiences and sent

shockwaves through the industry. The story, written by Javed Akhtar and Salim Khan, centres around the adventures of two petty crooks Veeru and Jai, hired by a retired police chief to hunt down a notorious bandit. Such was the impact of the film that it ran for five consecutive years in Bombay, and sections of the dialogue (sold separately from the music on cassettes) were (and still are) recited almost as a mantra by the cinema-going population of India and the far-flung communities of the Indian diaspora. Scenes are still regularly parodied both in films and on TV, and a remake starring Bachchan's son Abishek Bachchan is in the pipeline.

During the 1970's, producer/director Yash Chopra, primarily associated with love stories and romantic intrigues, directed three hugely successful films of the newfound 'action' genre, *Deewar* (The Wall, 1975), *Trishul* (Trident, 1978) and *Kaala Pathar* (Black Stone, 1979), all of which championed the cause of the working man's hero and affirmed the iconic status of Amitabh Bachchan.

The elements of *dhishoom dhishoom** introduced in the films of the 1970's form a part of the *masala* (spice-mix) of many contemporary films. Their importance is reaffirmed as the list of remakes from the decade of The Emergency, which transformed the film hero from middle class romantic to working class angry young man, like that of the films of the 1950's and 1960's, is lengthening by the year.

During the 1980's and 1990's, several forces were at play politically within the media framework of India, and concerning the target audience for Hindi movies, which brought about operational and genre changes within the industry. Unlike in other countries with a large-scale film industry, television posed no threat to Indian cinema until 1982 when its transmission became more widespread. Yet even as late as 1987, television sets were so thin on the ground that whole neighbourhoods would huddle around a single set to watch the Sunday morning episode of the dramatisation of the Hindu epic the *Ramayana,* which ran for 78 weeks.

* derived from the sound effects used in movie fight scenes, *dhishoom dhishoom* has become a phrase in Bombay/Hindi movie slang to describe on-screen violence)

Left: Film poster for Mother India.

The arrival of cable television, which unofficially began in 1984, brought films into the domestic arena, and began to lure audiences away from the cinema. By 1990, more than 3,000 cable operators were in operation across India, bringing to viewers a selection of anything from 10–50 channels where previously there had only been one, the state-run Doordharshan.

The film industry had to adapt to the change of operating environment, from enjoying a monopoly on the exhibition of films, to being thrust into competition with cable companies, often with scant regard for copyright infringement. Even today, despite police crackdowns and increased regulations, it is not uncommon for cable operators to air pirated copies of movies still showing at the cinema or even prior to their official release. Soap operas, game shows and lifestyle programmes offer alternative sources of entertainment, keeping audiences at home.

However, for the most part, a mutually beneficial relationship has developed between the cable and film industries, opening up new streams of revenue for both. Cable operators pay highly for the telecast rights to popular films, while at the same time they are able to cash in on the broadcasting of award ceremonies, film music videos, celebrity gossip and celebrity hosted shows. The cable and satellite networks have also provided the film industry with a valuable advertising platform for new releases, as well as increasing the exposure of Hindi films and *filmi* culture overseas.

The late 1980's and 1990's saw a massive increase in the filming of Hindi movies at locations outside India, a trend set in motion in the early 1980's. The ongoing insurgency in Kashmir, which began in 1989, rendered the Himalayan state's fragrant mountains, dreamy lakes and perfumed gardens, once the backdrop for scores of romantic interludes and song sequences, too dangerous for filmmakers to risk.

One of the first directors to make the move and shoot outside India was Yash Chopra, whose choices of foreign locations have proved popular with Indian audiences, and have gained him prestige overseas. The Swiss government awarded him for his contribution to the tourist industry, and there is even a lake in Switzerland used by Chopra as a location, now popularly known as Chopra Lake.

The shifting of a large portion of the shooting of Hindi films to foreign locations also helped to broaden the target audience for Bollywood movies. Many Hindi filmmakers now produce films with the foreign market in mind, opening distribution centres in major cities around the world, and dubbing and subtitling films into several languages enabling them to cater to global audiences outside the South Asian diaspora. While Hindi films have been exported and screened overseas since the 1930's, it is only recently that filmmakers have drawn any real earnings from overseas sales.

However, the fact that only certain types of Hindi films enjoy international success has led to a change in the dominant themes and types of hero portrayed in Bollywood films. In turn, this has lead to accusations by the Indian media that filmmakers are now producing movies according to the tastes of overseas markets, while ignoring the preferences of domestic audiences.

The year 1994 saw the release of *Hum Apke Hain Kaun?* (HAHK), (Who Am I to You?), which despite being slammed as a flop after preview screenings, went on to become the highest grossing Indian film of all time, joining *Sholay* as one of the films still screened somewhere in India today. Leading filmmaking trends away from the angry, violence driven era, *HAHK* paved the way for wholesome love stories, exalting family values and traditions dominant in contemporary Bollywood. Aside from establishing a new direction, *HAHK* succeeded in luring families back to the cinema, which during the previous era had been male dominated territory, and introduced the elaborate, stylised wedding as a staple component in films thereafter.

The new trend of filmmaking was further cemented in 1995 with the release of *Dilwale Dulhania Le Jayenge* (DDLJ), (The One With the True Heart Wins the Bride). Continuing the emphasis on traditional values, extensive use of foreign locations, fused with hearty doses of Punjabi culture, it was also the first contemporary Hindi movie to focus on Indians living overseas. *DDLJ*, in affirming the notion that westernisation need not be at odds with Indian identity, became a huge success both in the newly liberalised India, and with audiences of the South Asian diaspora. In May 2005, *DDLJ* marked its 500th week of matinee shows, making it the longest running movie in the country with the world's biggest film industry.

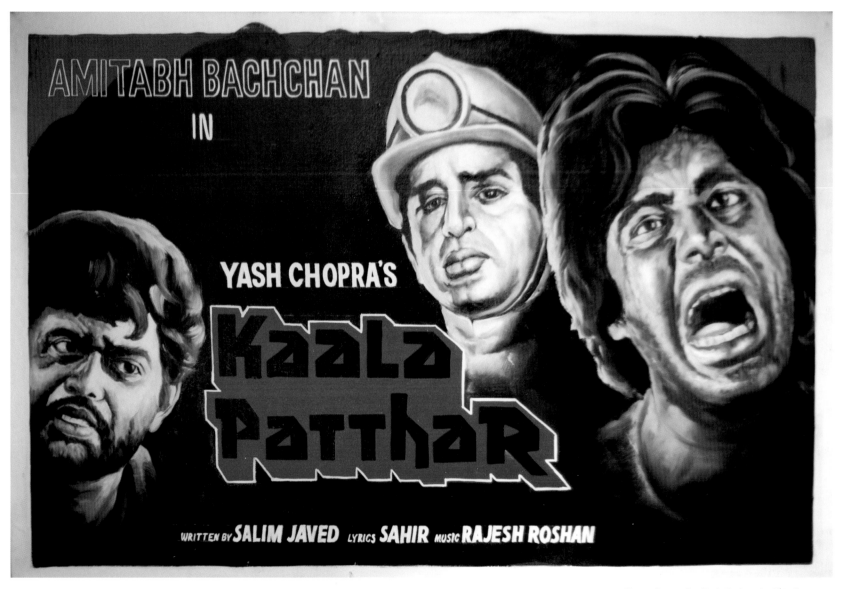

Above: Poster for Kaala Pathar, the film that
affirmed the iconic status of Amitabh Bachchan.

Left: A simple cinema ticket, or a magic charm capable of transporting the bearer to a world of dreams and glamour.

Gone are the days of the working man's hero, as all traces of economic hardship are wiped away from the lavish sets upon which the movies are filmed. The family and the hero portrayed in Bollywood movies since the mid-1990's, the decade that saw the creation of an Indian middle-class, are now extremely wealthy. The story of love transcending social boundaries has also largely been consigned to history, while the traditions surrounding cultural events and celebrations such as weddings and festivals have experienced a revival and are often the platform for the most elaborate costumes and dance scenes of the film.

Although films dealing with both patriotism and organised crime had been previously explored, during the 1990's both were redefined to reflect the times, their new incarnations becoming prevailing themes and roles in contemporary Bollywood.

Satya, released in 1998, although achieving more critical acclaim than large-scale commercial success, set the standard for the new 'gangster' represented in Bollywood movies. In a departure from earlier films dealing with the world of organised crime, *Satya,* directed by Ram Gopal Varma, offered a thought provoking, de-glamorised view of the Bombay underworld, presenting gangsters in a more humane light while continuing to portray politicians and police as ineffectual and corrupt. The film set new standards for the genre and initiated a spate of Bombay gangster movies.

Patriotism and nationhood was by no means a new theme explored by Bombay filmmakers, but ever since the 1990's, what patriotism involves and requires has been of a different essence from that portrayed in earlier films. *Mother India,* an empassioned socialist-inspired call for patience, virtue and faith in the future, was reflective of the prevailing social and political conditions of the time. Yet by the mid-90's, the patriotism represented in films had become a celebration of cultural identity and economic success to reflect the climate of economic liberalisation.

In 2001, Bollywood entered a new level in the world arena, becoming more high profile and even trendy and influential. In that year *Lagaan* (Land Tax), produced by and starring Aamir Khan, in a near four-hour spectacle infused with song, dance and traditional costumes, combined elements of patriotism and the triumph of the underdog, binding them together with a plot surrounding a game of cricket, India's other national passion aside from Bollywood. With songs and dialogue in both Hindi and English the film was obviously aimed at a wider audience. Aside from scooping up a number of national and international awards, *Lagaan* was the first Bollywood movie to truly break through on a large scale with worldwide audiences beyond the diasporic communities.

Aside from the overseas success of *Lagaan* and English language films presenting elements of Indian life and culture such as Mira Nair's *Monsoon Wedding* (2001) and Gurinder Chadha's *Bend It Like Beckham* (2002), Bollywood has begun to make inroads into Hollywood movies and western popular culture. Hollywood director, Baz Luhrman, makes no pretence about the influence of Bollywood aesthetics and production values on his 2001 spectacular *Moulin Rouge.* Terry Zwigoff's *Ghost World,* released the same year, paid tribute to Bollywood's rock 'n' roll years, placing a song and dance sequence from *Gumnaam* (1966) in a musical collage that also includes UK Post-Punk band, The Buzzcocks, and Blues legend, Skip James. *Bombay Dreams, the Musical* staged by Andrew Lloyd Webber and Indian composer A.R. Rahman opened in 2002 to rave reviews and is still going strong.

On the screen, the stage, in fashion and music, the world continues to awaken to the Bollywood vibe. Hindi movies, emerging from their own indigenous cinematic heritage and culture, are assuming a more significant role in global popular culture. Drawing an ever-increasing number of converts to the trademark song and dance spectaculars emanating from Bombay, the film capital of the world has proved itself to be the most prolific film producing nation.

Left: A statue of 'The Father of Indian Cinema', Dadasaheb Phalke stands outside a studio at the Film City shooting facility on the outskirts of Bombay. He produced the first Indian feature film, *Raja Harishchandra*, in 1913.

Music in Motion

Mention the name of a Bollywood movie to a devotee of Hindi cinema, and rather than evoking a slice of dialogue, or a description of a scene, he or she will invariably burst into one of the songs 'picturised' in the film. In Hollywood, musicals are classed as a separate genre, yet in Bollywood no such classification exists as virtually every film would be termed as a musical in the West. A film without song and dance routines is generically labelled as an art film, as the omission of these elements is deemed as being outside the accepted norms of the mainstream industry.

The use of music and dance in drama has its roots in Indian culture as far back as the Sanskrit theatre of ancient India. From the Jashn of Kashmir in the north to the Kathakali of Kerala in the south, through every region of the subcontinent and every phase of its history, song and dance have been an integral part of story-telling. The tradition is so deeply engrained that it is virtually impossible to imagine a performance without the inclusion of these two potent, vibrant ingredients of Indian culture. With the advent of sound in the Bombay film industry and *Alam Ara* (Beauty of the World), the first Indian talkie in 1931, the thread remained unbroken and Indian dramatic tradition carried on in the new medium.

Often acting as a kind of interlude in the main setting of the film, dance sequences frequently escape from the confines of the movie to far-flung locations or different sets and actors miraculously appear in different costumes. Although far from being unconnected to the story, song and dance sequences are an essential part of the narrative, forming bridges between sections of the film, which, if removed, would render the plot incomprehensible.

Right: Students of traditional *Kathak* dance go through their practice steps at a dance school in the Juhu suburb of Bombay. Although the role of classical Indian dance is diminishing in Bollywood movies, elements of many contemporary routines featured in the movies have at least one foot in the classics.

Dance scenes also satisfy the longings of an audience, which, in compliance with Indian censorship laws and codes of morality, filmmakers cannot depict in the conventional sense. In Indian films, scenes involving kissing have been traditionally banned, so the function of explicit or overtly sexual scenes in European and American movies is fulfilled by the expression of passion through song and dance, often with a more erotic effect.

The poetic traditions with which Hindi film songs are infused enable film-makers to deal with complex emotional issues which dialogue would take much longer to evoke, and would leave the appetites of audiences unabated. Song and dance routines, therefore, are invested with enormous importance, as they are quintessentially the deciding factor between a box office hit and a flop.

Since the 1950's, dance in Hindi movies has mainly been more reminiscent of Broadway than *Bharata Natyam* (a form of classical dance which originated in South India), and is viewed by traditionalists as the death or degeneration of Indian classical dance traditions. Elements of classical dance still feature in period films and a number of contemporary actors and actresses have received training in one school or another of traditional Indian dance.

For the majority of Indians, however, classical dance is as remote to them as ballet is to the majority of Europeans and Americans, and as such, their ideas about music and dance are formed by what they see and hear in films. Dance sequences portrayed in films have drawn influence from the twist and jive of the 1950's and 1960's, disco of the 1970's and 1980's to low-slung hip-hop swaggering in recent years, yet all the while the overall effect has remained purely Bollywood.

Recent years have seen the emergence of a new song and dance trend in Bollywood, whereby the main sequence is held in the context of a wedding or cultural event, incorporating traditional regional folk dances such as *Garba*

Right: A dancer from a Russian troupe adjusts the costume of her colleague in between shots on a set constructed for the movie *Hum Ko Deewana Kar Gaye*.

Opposite: Actor Mahesh Thakur (L) and actress Bhagyashree (R) strut their stuff in a dance routine during the filming of *Hum Ko Deewana Kar Gaye*.

Choreographer Geeta Kapur surveys the dance floor prior to the filming of a dance sequence for the movie *Pyare Mohan* on a set at Filmistan Studios.

from the state of Gujarat and the Punjabi *Bhangra*. This element has proved very popular with audiences of the South Asian diaspora who left India with what they could carry of their culture and memories packed in their suitcases.

Throughout India, speakers at music stands rattle and cough as they pour out an endless stream of film music. Released in advance of the films themselves, it is well understood that good songs will go a long way to making the film a success at the box office. Film music accounts for 80 per cent of total music sales in India, meaning that any walk or drive through an Indian town or city is likely to occur to the accompaniment of layer upon layer of Bollywood film songs, emanating from homes, shops and vehicles of varying shapes and sizes. The advent of widely available cable TV in India brought with it a whole host of game shows, which test contestants on their knowledge of film songs, or on their ability to re-enact and perform them.

Film songs have even been the subject of parliamentary debate, most notably in 1993 following the release of *Choli Ke Peeche Kya Hai?* (What is behind my blouse?) from the film *Khalnayak* (Villain). The song sparked widespread protest, which led to a debate in parliament over the possible banning of the song. Such controversy, perhaps not surprisingly, served only to further promote the film and its soundtrack, making it a bigger hit at the box office than it already was.

From weddings to funerals, and from religious festivals to political conventions, the film song has pervaded every aspect of Indian life.

In Bombay, the experience intensifies as street children spring into impromptu dance routines at the sound of the latest *filmi* hit. Flute sellers, loitering youths and mobile phone ring tones fill the air with constant renditions. Even sex-workers in Kamathipura, the city's notorious red-light district, lure clients to the strains of film music. The film song also takes the place of the wolf-whistle as young men sing unabashed of the beauty or their intentions towards passing girls. Couples courting surreptitiously in the evening shadow of the Gateway of India seem to adopt the virtuous mannerisms of the more delicate song sequences associated with the bittersweet joys of courtship in Bollywood films.

Star of the 1960's, Shammi Kapoor, says of film music, "I was always driven by music, when I performed the way I acted was always in response to the music I was hearing... But more than that I would say that, as a star, I was incomplete without the voice of Mohammed Rafi, and in some way I feel that I acted as a mouthpiece, enabling him, a quiet, humble man, to sing the outrageous songs that he recorded for me to perform."

Playback singing sisters, Lata Mangeshkar and Asha Bhosle, who, between them, have provided the singing voices for virtually every leading lady from 1948 to the present day, also have their favourites. "I loved to see Madhubala performing

Right: A sign advertising western dance classes at a dance school in Bombay. The city is brimming with aspiring actors, directors, writers and dancers, while others make a living by providing courses for young hopefuls.

to my songs," says the nightingale of India, Lata Mangeshkar. "She was so beautiful and you really felt that it was her singing, not me, the same was also true of Hema Malini."

Despite remaining physically in the shadows, Lata's fame and prominence in the industry has outlived that of many whom she has performed for. Several contemporary actresses have remarked that they felt their acceptance into the industry came when they added the on-screen dimension to a song by Lata. Even Bollywood actor and current heartthrob Shah Rukh Khan is quoted as having said, "I wish I had been an actress and to have had the honour to perform a song sung by Lataji on screen."

Her younger sister, Asha Bhosle, who famously completed the on-screen persona of Helen, Indian cinema's favourite dancer and star of more than 500 films, says of their relationship, "She (Helen) would bring chocolates for me at the recording studio and ask me very sweetly to remember that it was her I was singing for... I knew just what she meant and so I would put all those touches into my recording."

Through collaborations with 80's British pop-icon Boy George, and more recently with New York

ensemble Kronos Quartet, Asha has succeeded in spreading the gospel of Hindi film music to audiences worldwide. Through their distinctive singing styles, the sisters have given voice to two sides of morality dealt with in Hindi films. Lata's high-pitched, impeccably pure and ethereal voice is used to instil chaste virtue in the heroine, while Asha's sizzling, more gutsy, yet flawless tones complete the sexualised allure of the vamp.

Film music has evolved with the years to reflect of the trends that have swept through the subcontinent. From *Bhajans* (Hindu devotional songs) to *Bhangra, Ragas* (systems of music used in Indian Classical music) to rock 'n' roll and beyond, *filmi* music has taken in all forms of influence to come up with distinctive flavours of its own, while maintaining the lyrical traditions of Hindi and Urdu poetry. Luminaries such as the inimitable Shankarsinh Raghuwanshi and Jaikishan Dayabhai Pankal (Shankar-Jaikishan) partnership, Naushad, S.D. Burman, R.D. Burman, A.R. Rahman and lyricist and poet Javed Akhtar, have brought the film song through its various changes, phases and evolutions. Love songs, patriotic anthems, songs of the pain of separation and the joys of being reunited, as visible as Bollywood is, are all equally audible.

Right: Dance instructor Rajeshree Shirke (L) corrects the posture of a student in her *Kathak* dance class in the Juhu suburb of Bombay.

Opposite: The feet of a student of *Kathak* dance become a blur as she goes through her practice at a dance school.

Left: Students of traditional *Bharatha Natyam* dance are put through their practice steps by teacher Vaibhav Arekar (in pink shirt) at a dance school.

Left: Actress and dancer, Helen, gives life to a song as actors Akshay Kumar (L) and Upasana Singh (C) look on during the filming of *Hum Ko Deewana Kar Gaye* at Filmistan Studios. Helen, her on-screen persona completed by the voice of playback singer Asha Bhonsle, danced her way through scores of Bollywood films during the 1960's and 1970's, and is experiencing something of a comeback.

Dancers from a Russian troupe rehearse their moves on a set for the movie *Hum Ko Deewana Kar Gaye*.

Playback singer, Asha Bhonsle, records a song at a studio in suburban Bombay. In a career spanning over 50 years, Asha has been the voice of scores of actresses.

Playback singer, Lata Mangeshkar, gestures as she remembers the lyrics of an old hit. Lata is renowned in the country for her singing skills and is widely acknowledged as the nightingale of India.

Young students at a local dance school dance to the Bollywood beat during a party marking India's Independence Day.

Kathak dancer, Indrayanee Mukherjee, prepares for a rehearsal at her home. Many contemporary dance routines still contain elements of classical Indian dance.

Before the Camera

Bollywood actress Preity Zinta is the face of Pepsi in India. Star-studded advertising campaigns have become a feature of product promotion across India, with celebrities promoting all manner of goods, from fashion to fertiliser.

"Who is that actor? The one with a white beard and dark hair who you see everywhere," is a question frequently asked by visitors to India. "That is Mr. Amitabh Bachchan, the biggest star in Indian cinema," runs the reply, more often than not delivered in the hushed tones of something not too far removed from reverence. In the 1970's, the decade of disillusionment in India, Amitabh Bachchan popularised a new kind of hero far removed from the romantic heroes of earlier films. His portrayal of the angry young man burst onto the screen, capturing the box office, the spirit of the times and the empathy of a disaffected youth.

Born in Allahabad, in the northern Indian state of Uttar Pradesh, the son of the noted Hindi poet, Harivanshrai Bachchan, Amitabh Bachchan rose to iconic status in 1973 with the film *Zanjeer* (Chains) after a series of flops had him ready for a return to his hometown. Bachchan's place in the Bollywood Pantheon was sealed with his role in the now legendary 'curry western', *Sholay* (Flames) released in 1975. In 1982, the nation all but came to a standstill after 'The Big B', as he is referred to in the Indian media, suffered a near fatal accident during shooting for the film *Coolie*. The media issued regular bulletins on his condition and even the then Prime Minister Indira Gandhi cut short her visit to the US to return home. Following his recovery, the film was released featuring a freeze-frame and caption, enabling fans to identify the exact point in time of his injury.

'The Big B' phenomenon is something incredible, as stars normally wax and wane in an industry where films are more reliant on stars than stories to woo audiences, and in a country where being a star means becoming part of a Pantheon to be revered by the masses.

Ever the perfectionist, Bollywood megastar Amitabh Bachchan takes a hands-on approach to his hairstyling before going for a take in the movie *Baabul* (Father's House).

Such is his status that his face adorns billboards all over the country as advertisers use his image to promote a whole range of products, from pens to paints. His make-up artist of 35 years, Deepak Sawant has become something of a celebrity and even Gulzar Mallayanor, reputedly Bachchan's biggest fan, is frequently featured in TV shows and magazines. In 1999, a BBC on-line poll confirmed Bachchan's iconic status when he was voted 'Star of the Millennium', beating the likes of Sir Lawrence Olivier, Sir Alec Guinness, Charlie Chaplin, Cary Grant and Robert De Niro.

"Magic happens when he appears before the camera," said producer Keshu Ramsay during shooting for the film *Family: Ties of Blood*. "He knows instinctively what the role requires of him and he does exactly that."

When Amitabh Bachchan arrives on a set, the crew and cast standing as bodyguards announce his arrival. When shooting is complete and he heads for his trailer, word has already spread and he is greeted by adoring fans.

Even today, more than 30 years after the success of *Zanjeer*, Bachchan, who also hosts *Kaun Banega Crorepati?*, the Indian version of the TV game show *Who Wants To Be A Millionaire?*, continues to be probably the busiest actor in Bollywood. With parts still written especially for him, he is the one actor who has remained a star as he advanced in years as opposed to being sidetracked into cameos and character roles.

Of Amitabh Bachchan's contemporaries, actress Hema Malini, who appeared alongside him in *Sholay* (Flames, 1975), has retained much of her star value, and in recent years has been cast opposite Bachchan as they play the roles of stylish yet traditional parents. "She (Hema Malini) always asks me how I manage to keep her looking beautiful whenever I film her," says cinematographer Barun Mukherjee, "and I have to say to her that every time I see her through the camera, it's like falling in love all over again."

Right: Actors Vivek Oberoi (R) and Fardeen Khan (2-R) run through a shot as final lighting measurements are taken prior to the filming of a sequence for the movie *Pyare Mohan* at Filmistan Studios.

Like many Bollywood stars, including her actor husband Dharmendra, Hema Malini has ventured into politics, becoming a member of the Bharatiya Janata Party (BJP) and of the Rajya Sabha, India's Upper House of Parliament. The blurring of the line between movie star and politician is neither a rarity nor exclusive to Bollywood. Yet the power of the star in India makes the arranged marriage between the two beneficial for both, as the alignment of a star with a political party either through membership or support, can draw crowds to rallies and support for parties like no politician ever could.

Of the younger generation of actors, Aamir Khan is among the best-known outside India and the South Asian diaspora, as he was probably the first Bollywood star many people saw in action in the worldwide hit, *Lagaan*. He is also one of the highest regarded actors in the Bombay film industry. In *Lagaan*, Khan played the role of a fictional villager who stood up against the imposition of an unjust tax by British authorities, although his method of fighting back was on the cricket pitch rather than the battlefield.

In his latest film *Mangal Pandey–The Rising* (released August 2005), he portrays Mangal Pandey, one of the main players in the real-life Indian Mutiny of 1857. Despite his enormous successes in these two heroic, anti-imperialist roles, Aamir Khan is keen to point out that both the themes dealt with, in *Lagaan* and *Mangal Pandey–The Rising*, and the characters he plays in them, must be viewed on a broader level. "First and foremost I am an entertainer, my aim is primarily to entertain and not to raise social issues. In *Lagaan,* the character of Bhuvan was not essentially a nationalistic character. He did not hate the British and did not want to drive them out of India. He was simply an underdog who stood up against injustice. The theme is more universal than simply Nationalistic... *Mangal Pandey–The Rising,* in essence, covers a much broader theme than simply the Indian mutiny; that of people aspiring to decide upon their own destiny and empowering themselves to do so."

Left: Actress Hema Malini shares a light-hearted moment while rehearsing her lines on the set of the film *Baabul*.

Right: Actor Vivek Oberoi offers prayers before the camera prior to the start of a day's shooting on a set constructed for the movie *Pyare Mohan*.

Mangal Pandey–The Rising, opened in August 2005, and despite criticism from both British and Indian historians for historical inaccuracies, it drew critical acclaim and strong box office sales both in India and overseas.

The current poster-boy of Bollywood among domestic and diasporic audiences is actor Shah Rukh Khan. Even Amitabh Bachchan proclaimed during a TV interview in October 2005, "I am not the *badshah* (king) of the film industry. I am only a member. Shah Rukh Khan is the *badshah*."

Rising to the peak of the industry in 1995 with his performance in *Dilwale Dulhaniya Le Jayenge* (DDLJ), (The One With The True Heart Wins The Bride), Khan emerged from a background in theatre and television as well as a number of unconventional film roles. Khan has played a variety of characters from comic to killer, working class to wealthy, yet it is for his roles as the sensitive, cosmopolitan hero of *DDLJ*, *Kuch Kuch Hota Hai* (Something Happens, 1998), *Kabhie Khushi Kabhi Gham* (Sometimes There Is Happiness, Sometimes There Is Sorrow, 2001) and a string of hits in similar roles, that he is best known. Although in recent years Khan has reduced his workload in films, his work in advertising appears to have stepped up a gear as TV commercials and poster campaigns of him appear in profusion all over India. He has become part of the landscape and keeps his place warm in the crowded Pantheon of stars in between films.

The demands on Bollywood stars are incredible, as the disjointed nature of the production process dictates that they work on several productions at the same time. As a result actors notch up a staggering amount of work in a relatively short period. Muscle-bound actor, Salman Khan, has appeared in almost double the number of films in half the number of years as Hollywood muscleman Arnold Schwarzenegger, and Amitabh Bachchan has starred in four times as many films as Al Pacino in a career of similar length.

Even more than in Hollywood, in Bollywood it's the stars that can make or break a film. Privileged and exclusive their status may be, but on the

Opposite: Actor Shah Rukh Khan speaking to media representatives during a press conference.

Left: Actor Aamir Khan gestures as he speaks during an interview at MTV studios in Bombay.

whole, stars of the Bombay film industry remain surprisingly accessible and ultimately susceptible to the nature of their city.

Their cars, although air-conditioned and chauffeur driven, still get stuck in the gnarling traffic jams and are mobbed at every junction by magazine vendors and beggars. Their homes, although bearing all the hallmarks of the opulence their trade affords them, still fall victim to the power-cuts that plague Indian cities. On set and location they pick their way through the grime, eating not from groaning buffet tables, but standard Indian fare. In between shots they sit on moulded plastic patio seats as opposed to personalised slung canvas directors' chairs. In the case of Amitabh Bachchan, three such chairs are routinely stacked and lashed together as part of set preparations for him, affording the 6 foot 3 inch tall star the maximum comfort from available resources.

Perhaps it is these images of stars seemingly sharing the habits and hardships of the city that seals the status of Bollywood icons among audiences who adore the fantastical world they inhabit on the screen, yet appreciate any hint at inner simplicity. Though the stars of Bollywood appear god-like on giant billboards, looming large over the skyline of Bombay, as much as they reign over the city, in the eyes of their fans they are still part of it.

Left: The star-studded cast of *Baabul*, Amitabh Bachchan (L), Hema Malini (2-L), Salman Khan (2-R) and Rani Mukherjee (R) rehearse a sequence on a set constructed for the film at the Film City shooting facility on the outskirts of Bombay.

Actor Salman Khan poses for a photograph during shooting for the movie *No Entry* at a hotel in a Bombay suburb.

Actress Katrina Kaif checks her hair and make-up on the set of the movie *Hum Ko Deewana Kar Gaye* filmed at Filmistan Studios.

Actor Akshay Kumar (centre) and his co-stars Gurpreet Guggi (R) and Vivek Shauq (L) on the set of *Hum Ko Deewana Kar Gaye*.

Actress Rani Mukherjee runs through her lines with director Ravi Chopra on the set of the film *Baabul*.

A Look Through the Lens

In films the world over, the hidden craft of the cinematographer is often taken for granted by audiences who concentrate on the performance of stars and possibly the work of the director. Cinematographers working in the Bombay film industry are up against difficulties their European and American counterparts could scarcely comprehend. Dust, heat, floods and gawking crowds seemingly conspire to make the work harder for those behind the camera. When shooting in the streets of Bombay, cinematographers operate almost in the manner of news cameramen in cinematic smash and grab raids on the city, as guards simply pull back the crowds with ropes as the shot is taken.

Though renowned for lavish, glossy production values, Bollywood films are shot utilising minimal technology, more often than not with just a single camera unit, improvised lighting equipment and manually operated dollies and cranes. Add to that the frustrations, delays and consistency issues involved in disjointed shooting schedules with actors working on several films simultaneously,

and the work of Bombay lens men becomes even more remarkable. Yet the polish of the finished product offers no perceivable hint of the conditions Bollywood cinematographers work under.

Cinematographer Sunil Patel, whose work on the 2005 hit *Salaam–Namaste* drew praise from all quarters, says of the difficulties experienced by cinematographers working in Bollywood, "It's a constant battle, the dust gets everywhere even when you're working on a set, these poor guys (pointing to the team of cleaners) have a never ending job, and it's tough keeping the stuff out of the camera. When you're out on location here it's even more difficult, then you have the dust, the heat and the crowds to deal with. It's tough but I think in the end it makes you better at the job you do. I studied at film school in London, but it's here that I really learned my craft."

In the Bombay film industry, rags to riches stories are becoming thinner on the ground as stars and directors increasingly emerge from cinematic dynasties, and cinematographers come via the more formal route of film school.

Left: Cinematographer Sunil Patel gives instructions to crew members during shooting for the film *Pyare Mohan* at Filmistan Studios.

Ashok Mehta, one of the most sought-after cinematographers in India, ran away from home in Delhi at age 14, working for a hawker selling boiled eggs as his first job upon arrival in Bombay. In 1963, while selling watermelon slices, he watched a film shoot and became hooked. Working his way up from canteen boy at one studio, to office boy in another, then part-time studio hand, up through the ranks of camera attendant to eventually becoming cinematographer on Raj Marbros' *The Witness* in 1974. Although the film never made it beyond initial stages, Mehta's work on *The Witness* impressed star of the 1970's Shashi Kapoor, who offered him the cinematographers job on his next production *36 Chowringhee Lane*. From then on Mehta's career has gone from strength to strength, both in the parallel cinema movement and in the mainstream industry. His presence on a shoot charges the crew with a sense of urgency, his hands-on approach and intense concentration igniting the atmosphere as he goes.

"Cut!"… "I shouted 'Action' and she didn't move," was a phrase used by Mehta during shooting for the film *No Entry* in a Bombay hotel foyer, which truly encapsulates the essence of the notorious powerhouse. Mehta, whose work on the 1995 film *Bandit Queen* won international acclaim, is renowned for his hands-on approach, and for slipping into the director's role when necessity calls. He is also known for his ability to light up a scene in a matter of minutes, knowing exactly what to use and where, "I prefer to take my time to light up, but in shooting mainstream films there is never enough time ... But too much time can be a bad thing, because then you end up wasting time and there is nothing worse than that."

Right: Renowned cinematographer Ashok Mehta sets up a shot during shooting for the film *Family: Ties of Blood*. Mehta, who began his career in the film industry as a canteen boy at one of the city's studios has gone on to become one of the leading cinematographers in Bollywood.

Barun Mukherjee, whose list of credits as a cinematographer includes the hugely successful Amitabh Bachchan–Hema Malini film, *Baghban* (Gardener: 2003) and internationally acclaimed *The Speaking Hand: Zakir Hussain and the Art of the Indian Drum* (2003), although entering the film industry after studying at the Film and Television Institute of India (FTII), he first had to appease his father. "I had decided to apply for FTTI, but knew that my father would take some convincing as although he was very musically minded, he wanted his sons to become qualified engineers. My brother-in-law, who my father was very fond of, came to the rescue and did the talking for me, telling my father that I was applying for a course in sound engineering in Pune. The mere use of the word engineering was my trump card. It made him happy to some extent. I finally put in my application for sound engineering as the first preference and motion picture photography as the second."

While shooting on set, Mukherjee exudes a more patient and philosophical view of the hardships of his trade, "When I think it is getting tough down here, I look at those guys up there (pointing towards the lighting crew balanced precariously on runner boards lashed together 20 feet above the shooting floor). Their job is tough, with no thanks, no credit and little pay. They stay up there in the heat, risking their necks to illuminate the set for me, the cinematographer, to capture."

Whether on set or on location cinematographers of the Bombay film industry perform miracles with limited resources. Working with others behind the scenes like teams of pearl divers or diamond miners, they delve into the depths to emerge with gems to be cut and polished into dazzling cinematic jewels. Turning restriction into virtue, they capture the glamour of the stars and settings, leaving no discernable trace of the sweat and dust they leave behind.

Left: Choreographer Ganesh Acharya (L) watches a playback of a dance sequence along with director Raj Kanwar (R) during filming for the movie *Hum Ko Deewana Kar Gaye* at Filmistan Studios in the Goregaon suburb of Bombay.

Right: Cinematographer Vikas Shivaram ponders a shot during filming for the movie *Hum Ko Deewana Kar Gaye*.

Cinematographer Vikas Shivaram (centre) shoots a dance sequence for the film *Hum Ko Deewana Kar Gaye* at Filmistan Studios.

Right: Cinematographer Barun Mukherjee (seated) surveys the scene as his assistant Sandeep Ghosal (holding microphone) issues instructions to crew members during filming for the film *Baabul*.

Below: Barun Mukherjee studied cinematography after first enrolling for a sound engineering course. Since the course contained the word 'engineer' he felt it would appease his parents.

From left to right:
Sound engineer Dilip Subramaniam mans the mixing desk as he listens to dialogue taking place during filming for the film *Baabul*.

Assistant Cameraman Sandeep Ghosal (R) and a technician take light readings on a set constrcted for the film *Baabul* at the Film City.

A member of the lighting crew clips shields around a spotlight prior to shooting on the set of *Baabul*.

Assistant to director Indra Kumar, Leena Tandon listens to his instruction during shooting for the film *Pyare Mohan*. Bombay is full of aspiring actors, writers and directors, young hopefuls such as Leena often gain experience on sets by working as directors assistants.

A car fitted with mounting brackets for lights and cameras moves into position during a location shoot.

Right: Bombay is brimming with young hopefuls aspiring to enter the world of Bollywood. Not surprisingly, a whole industry has developed catering to these hopefuls as others make their living offering training courses geared towards a career in cinema.

Bollywood Dream Makers

"As a director you need passion, because nothing else will keep you going," says director Anees Bazmee during shooting for the film *No Entry*. "When you wait in the rain for 15 days on a foreign location with producers calling you every five minutes asking what is happening, and you know that each day wasted is costing them a fortune... And then you jump into action the moment the weather changes; only passion for making movies will drive you on. I love my work, I couldn't do it otherwise."

Bazmee, with 51 films to his credit as a writer, began his cinematic career as a child artiste in Hindi films, and went on at the age of 16 to act as assistant director to Raj Kapoor on the film *Prem Rog* (Addicted to Love, 1982). "Almost everything I've achieved as a director is because of what I picked up from Raj Sahib. From him I learned that a director is nothing without passion and dedication."

Ravi Chopra, whose father, B.R. Chopra, and uncle, Yash Chopra, are both revered as legends and pioneers of Indian cinema, began his career in 1974 with *Zameer* (Conscience). But it was as the director of India's marathon television serial, the *Mahabharat*, based upon India's immortal ancient epic, which ran for 93 consecutive weeks and was viewed by a staggering 96 per cent of India's TV audience, that Chopra really earned his stripes.

On the set, Chopra's training at the hands of his father and uncle is all too evident as he tirelessly moves between one task and another, often moving outside the expected director's parameters to complete the work of others to his satisfaction. As one who grew up in one of Hindi cinemas great families there is something of a family atmosphere in the air during shooting. Younger stars refer to him as 'Ravi Uncle' as he runs through dialogue and scenes with them, while actors of his own age group apply the suffix *bhai* (brother) to his name. "A tense atmosphere is bad for everyone, so I always try to keep the atmosphere light yet productive," says Chopra.

One very striking feature of the vast majority of directors in the Bombay film industry is that

Right: Director Rajkumar Santoshi (R) gives last minute instructions to Bollywood megastar Amitabh Bachchan (L) prior to a shot during filming for *Family: Ties of Blood*.

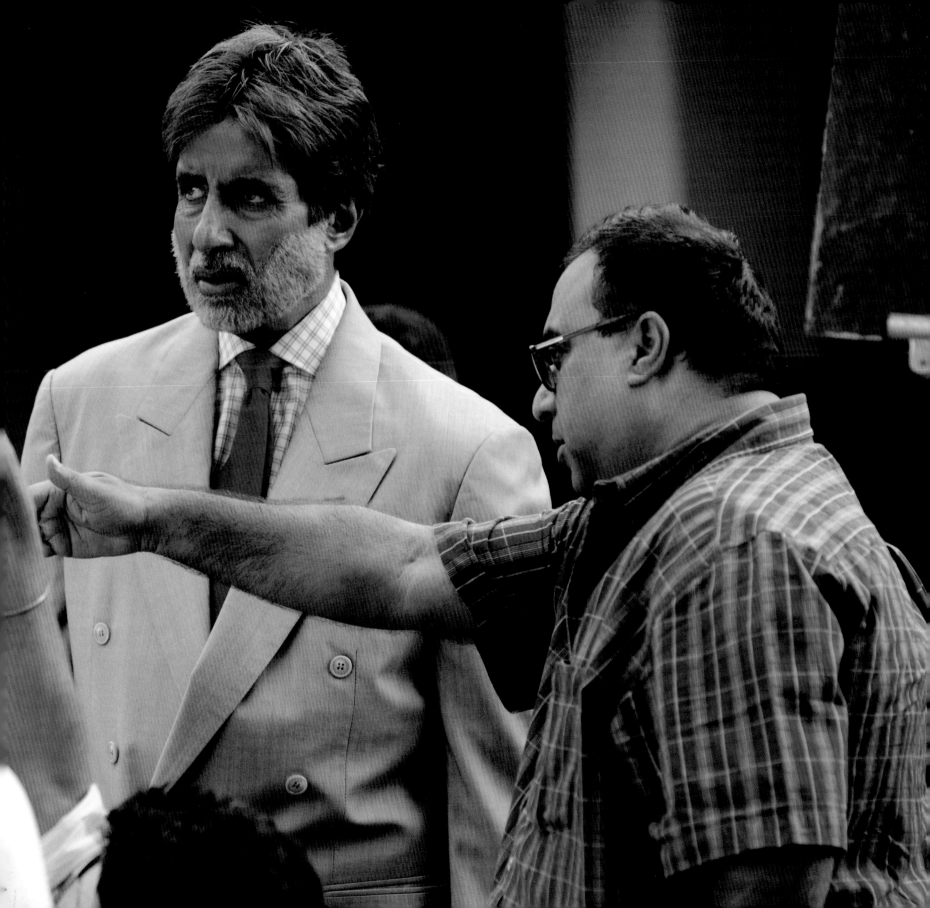

true to Bollywood form, they are the product of the industry, both in terms of their training and their influence. Their sense of aesthetics and vision are largely inspired by their predecessors and contemporaries in Indian cinema, and it is essentially they who preserve and develop that vision while adapting to the times and tastes of an ever expanding, ever changing audience.

Indra Kumar, younger brother of veteran actress Aruna Irani, made his directorial debut with the Saeed Jaffrey, Madhuri Dixit and Aamir Khan film *Dil* (Heart) in 1990. Emerging initially as a comedy actor in Gujarati movies, as a director he has become renowned in the industry for his leisurely approach to film making involving a lot of slashing and re-shooting scenes. "I like to let things happen sometimes, that way you get comedy and emotion that you don't get with too much interference... I like to grow with the film."

During shooting schedules his film-making formula becomes evident as he bounces between graphic instruction involving acting out scenes himself, and watching silently as his actors flesh out their characters and play out their scenes.

Left: Director Ravi Chopra issues instructions to crew members during shooting for the film *Baabul*.

Right: Director Indra Kumar (R) holds assistant director Dilip Halda (L) in a stranglehold as they demostrate a sequence to actors during filming for the movie *Pyare Mohan*.

The production of Hindi film is an extremely collaborative process in which directors are deeply involved from very early stages. The relationships built between director, cast and crew, and his or her handling of on set tensions are crucial throughout the pre-production and production phase of a movie. In Bollywood, contracts are largely verbal and based upon personal commitment. From the very inception of an idea the director takes on a multitude of tasks, from working with scriptwriters and music directors to luring the stars into the project by narrating scripts to them. Since storyboards are not generally used, it is the director who maintains the vision and feel of the film through its trials, tribulations and disjointed shooting schedules. Soothing frayed nerves and wounded egos, dealing with clumsy stagehands and impatient producers, Bollywood directors are essentially ship captains, charting courses, battling and harnessing the elements as the movie takes shape.

Left: Director Indra Kumar gestures to crew members during shooting for the film *Pyare Mohan*.

Director Anees Bazmee (R) maps out a shot for cinematographer Ashok Mehta (L) during shooting for the film *No Entry* at a hotel on the outskirts of Bombay.

Life on the Fringes

The city of Bombay is bursting with guards, waiters, drivers and cooks, who are writers, actors or singers simply earning their living as best they can until the day they are discovered. Needless to say, for the vast majority of them that day never dawns, yet outside the inner sanctum of Bollywood, the allure of the industry keeps alive the dreams of thousands of young and not so young hopefuls. Through its movies Bombay remains a city of promise and endless possibilities. Like a beacon it draws scores of people from all over India into its teeming heart. Dance classes, drama classes, camera, writing and editing courses are available in profusion all over the city, as others make a living feeding the hopes of Bollywood aspirants.

It is not uncommon to find a taxi driver with a self-penned screenplay or two stuffed in his pocket on the off chance that his passenger could turn out to be his entry ticket into the industry. Cafés reputedly frequented by Bollywood directors and producers are more often the haunts of budding writers and actors, pinning back their desperation with hopes of a chance encounter with someone who could change their lives forever. At times it seems that almost everyone in the city is just waiting for their break into the promised land of films. On the fringes of Bollywood exists an entire subculture of people eking out a living from the industry, or awaiting their big break.

With a yearly average of 150–200 movies emanating from Bombay, there is a constant need for suitable extras to appear in films, and a network of agents, coordinators and professional extras whose living depends on meeting those demands. In addition to the regulars, Western extras, for whom more often than not, appearing in a Bollywood movie is just part of their India experience, are recruited from the cheap hotels of the city's Colaba district. Appearing as

Cleaners battle against the grimy footprints left on the floor of a set by the cast and crew of *Pyare Mohan*. This set was constructed for the film at Filmistan Studios.

colonial officers or in the background of discotheque scenes and hotel foyers, American and European extras receive a fee of Rs.500 (US$12) plus lunch and train fare to and from the studios. "The problem with foreign extras is that they don't stay around long enough," says cinematographer Sunil Patel while shooting for *Pyare Mohan* (Dear Mohan) at Filmistan Studios in the Goregaon suburb of Bombay. "One of the costumes we are using for extras is a short blue glittery dress. Everyday I look at the dress, and everyday someone different is wearing it. One day she's fat, the next day she's thin, it's a good thing we don't strive for realism."

There is even a contingent of fair-skinned local extras, with lightened hair and eyebrows, appearing as ersatz Westerners when the continuity demands or the shooting schedule requires more time than the average gap-year backpacker can afford.

Although there is a definite hierarchy amongst extras, with differentiations in pay and conditions, once on the set they all endure the same long hours under the heat and glare of the studio lights. Despite the fact that the passage from extra to star is extremely uncommon, a sense of hopefulness radiates from their numbers as each in turn tries to catch the eye of the director, investing energy and effort into their largely irrelevant parts, which the camera is not even focused to detect.

S.K. Abbas is an aspiring actor with a foot in the door. "I have been personal fitness trainer to Salman Khan, Anil Kapoor and Bipasha Basu," says Abbas, whose physique, taut and toned with free weights and gym equipment, betrays a distinctly Western influence; while the self flagellation scars on his back gained during the Shiite Muslim festival of Muharram offer clear confirmation of his religious background and conviction,. "I had a small part in *No Entry* (released in August 2005) and *Inshallah* (God Willing), I hope to make it as a star myself."

People become involved in the Bombay film industry in a variety of ways, some through formal training and education, some through connections, while

Right: Whether filming on location or in the studio, a lot of hard work and planning is required as everything from cameras to fans are moved manually.

Opposite: Members of the lighting crew struggle against the elements as they set up lighting during shooting in a brief downpour in the streets of Bombay.

others enter the industry after working in television, advertising or theatre. The majority of directors, however, worked first as directors' assistants, learning their art in a hands-on manner and making valuable connections, the film set being a far better place to network than film school. "I loved the films of Raj Kapoor and decided that I wanted to become a director," says Leena Tandon, assistant to director Indra Kumar on the film *Pyare Mohan*. "I'm here now learning all I can, it's hard work but I love it."

Entry into the inner sanctum of the film industry is a salvation that many of the Bombay hopefuls never achieve, although a good number manage to make a living in bit parts, as extras and peripheral technicians or become involved in television and advertising. The same may be true in other film industries around the world, but the reality of Bombay, in all its grime and glory, and the largely nepotistic nature of the Hindi film industry, makes the struggle of Bollywood aspirants all the more poignant and difficult.

Right: A make-up artist works on actor Akshay Kumar between takes.

Opposite: Members of the technical crew position lights and diffusers prior to the commencement of shooting on a set.

Foreign extras from the UK enjoy a break between shooting on location at a hotel on the outskirts of Bombay. They are mainly recruited from the budget hotels frequented by backpackers in the Colaba district of Bombay. Unlike their Indian counterparts, they are mostly in it for the experience rather than the money or any real desire to make a career in Bollywood.

Left: Tanya, a young Russian woman travelling in India, rides the local train to a studio where she will perform as a dancing extra.

Above: An extra re-applies her lipstick in between
takes on the set of *Hum Ko Dewana Kar Gaye*.

Right: An extra grabs a short nap as she waits for
her scene to be shot. Working as an extra means
long and gruelling hours under hot studio lights.

Bollywood snapper Joe has travelled extensively throughout Asia, Africa and Europe while shooting location stills for Bollywood movies.

"I have been personal trainer to Salman Khan, Anil Kapoor and Bipasha Basu," says S. K. Abbas at his gym in Bandra. "Now I hope to enter movies myself."

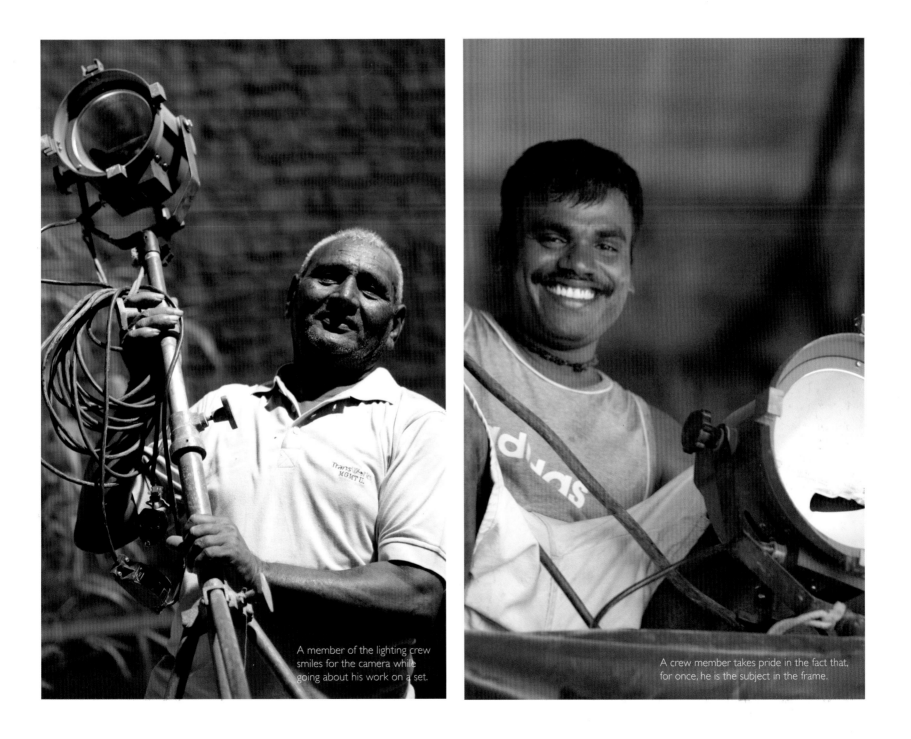

A member of the lighting crew smiles for the camera while going about his work on a set.

A crew member takes pride in the fact that, for once, he is the subject in the frame.

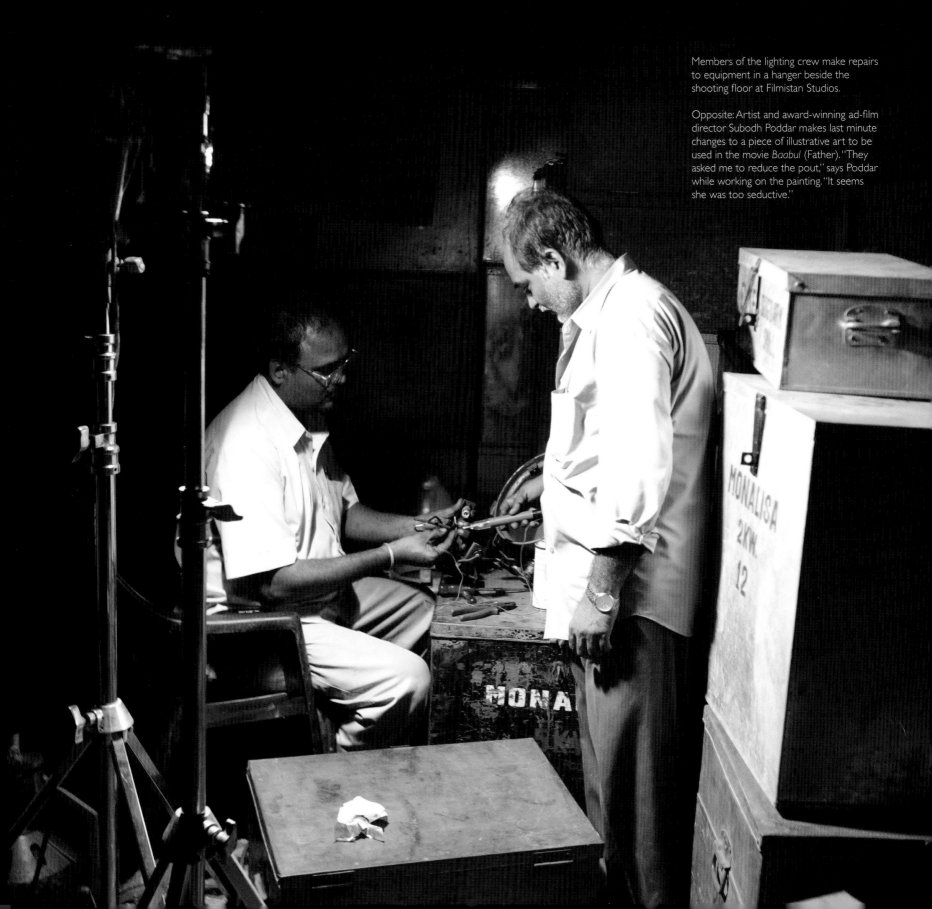

Members of the lighting crew make repairs to equipment in a hanger beside the shooting floor at Filmistan Studios.

Opposite: Artist and award-winning ad-film director Subodh Poddar makes last minute changes to a piece of illustrative art to be used in the movie *Baabul* (Father). "They asked me to reduce the pout," says Poddar while working on the painting. "It seems she was too seductive."

Above: Members of the lighting crew endure the heat and danger of working in the gantry suspended above a set.

Right: Keeping the costumes for extras clean and pressed is a never-ending job for staff in the wardrobe department.

Using basic tools and materials, tradesmen work to construct a set for the shooting of a Bollywood film at Filmistan Studios. Out of plywood and paint rise beautiful sets that are full of the glitz and glamour associated with Bollywood.